Want to know
nature

All About Dogs

Jozua Douglas & Hiky Helmantel

Clavis

NEW YORK

"Dad, I want a dog," Lana says.
She's been nagging for days now.
"Who will feed him?" Daddy asks.
"Who will take him for a walk?
Who will brush his teeth?"
"Me," Lana says. "I'm very good at that."
"You can get a dog when you're older," Daddy says.
"Later today Grandpa is coming by with Duffy.
Then you can start practicing."

Here is grandpa. He has brought his poodle Duffy.
Duffy barks. She wags her tail and jumps up when
she sees Lana.
"I have a little surprise," Grandpa says.
"Tomorrow we'll go to the big fancy dog show.
We are going to dress up Duffy. Maybe she'll even be
the prettiest dog in the country. But first I'll read you
from this dog book."

Sssh. Listen to the quietest sounds you can hear. Dogs **hear** even more. They can hear your father's car when he's still far away from home. You can't hear a thing. But dogs hear him coming from miles away.

Dogs **see** the world differently than you. They see fewer colors. To them everything is grey, yellow and blue, and red things look green. You can see further than they do. Dogs don't see clearly in the distance – they only see blurry things moving.

When your next-door neighbor makes pancakes, you might be able to smell them. But can you also smell the pancakes on the other side of town? That's easy for dogs. They have **super keen noses**. If you try to hide from a dog he'll find you in a flash – using his nose.

What are dogs?

Dogs make good friends. They are sweet and loyal and think it's lovely to play together. They can live to be sixteen years old. That's very old for a dog. Those are grandpa- and grandma-dogs.

With their **whiskers** dogs feel how close to things they might be. That way they don't bump their heads.

Dogs have **sharp teeth** which they use to tear off pieces of meat.

With their **tongues**, dogs lick you when they think you're sweet – or when they are hungry. Dogs also use their tongues to lap up water. And when it's hot, they let their tongues hang out of their mouths to cool off.

With their **tails** dogs show they are happy or angry, scared or sad.

Did you know

dogs are part of the wolf family? A very very long time ago people started to let wolves live with them in their homes. The wolves became tame and house-trained and many different types of dogs came into being.

What do dogs say?

Dogs have their own language. They bark, growl, whine and howl. They wag their tails and sometimes they even pee to explain something. Do you want to learn how to understand dogs?

I am sad
Dogs howl and whine when they are sad.

I am scared
Dogs curl up into a ball when they are scared.
They put their tails between their legs.
Their ears are flattened against their heads.
Be careful when a dog is scared. Don't get
too close, because he might bite.

I am happy
Dogs bark whenever they are happy.
They wag their tails and jump around you in circles.

I am angry
Dogs growl when they are angry.
Their tails stand straight up in the air.
Their ears are turned to the front. They show
their teeth and make themselves bigger.
That's how they say: "Careful, or I'll bite."

You are in control

When dogs lie on their backs, they're saying:
"You're in control. I will do whatever you say."
Don't lie on your back when you play with a dog
because then he'll think he's in control.

How are you?

When a dog runs into another dog, they start sniffing
each other. That is how they get to know each other.
"Hi, *sniff sniff*, who are you? Are you a boy or a girl?
Where do you come from? Are you alright?
Or are you sick?" Dogs can smell
it all.

Dog letters

Dogs smell everything. That is how they get
to know things. Dog piddles are especially
interesting to them. They know exactly which
dog left the pee. Pee is sort of like a letter
a dog leaves behind for other dogs.
It says: "Hello, I was here!"

How do you take care of a dog?

Dogs can be sweet and fun. You can play with them endlessly,
but you also have to take care of them every day. *Phew*...that's a lot of work.
Dogs eat food twice a day from their own bowls.
They get dried or canned pet food and drink water.
Not from a glass, but from a water bowl.

Oh, they can look so sad when they see you eat.
They want to eat what you're eating.
But human food isn't good for them.
So don't give dogs human food,
especially no chocolate,
because that can be poisonous.
If a dog is good you can give him
a doggie treat.

Did you know a dog will think that he is the boss if he's allowed to sleep in his owner's bed?

Of course dogs can't sit on the toilet. That is why you have to take them outside. That's just one of the reasons why you have to walk your dog. Outside dogs can relieve themselves, they can run around and play, get exercise, and smell everything they see.

Before you take your dog outside, he has to wear a leash. Because without a leash he will follow everyone he meets.

Did you know there is a special sort of dog toothpaste? It has a delicious meat taste. Don't give your dog human toothpaste. It's not good for him.

You have to walk a dog three times a day. Even when it rains. Or when it is cold outside. Or when there is something good on television.

You have to comb or brush your dog once a week. Every now and then cut his nails. And brush his teeth every day. He can't do that himself of course. That is why you have to do it all for him.

Sometimes you have to bathe your dog, but only when he is very dirty. Soap is not good for his fur.

What can dogs learn?

Dogs can learn a lot of things. Some dogs even go to dog school. Of course they don't learn how to read and write. Or how to ride a bike or tie their shoes. Dogs learn different things.

They learn that they have to do what their owners tell them to do: "Sit. Lie. Come. Stay. To your basket!"

Did you know

if you want to pet a dog you don't know, you must ask the dog's owner if it's okay. Let the dog sniff your hand first. Then he'll know who you are. Start with his chin when you pet him.

They learn that they have to pee outside.

Dogs can also learn how to give a paw. Or to fetch a ball when you throw it. When your dog does well you can give him a dog treat!

What do dogs love?

Dogs love playing. They love running, swimming, digging, exploring, jumping and playing around.
They like to run after you and retrieve things you throw. If you have a dog, let him chew on a tasty bone.
Give him his own ball. Pet him often, especially on his belly, he likes that best.

What do dogs hate?

Dogs don't like to be hugged. It scares them and they could bite.
Don't stare at a dog either, or run towards him. Dogs don't like loud noises
and they hate being interrupted when they are eating or enjoying a nice nap.

Did you know
you shouldn't run away
if you don't feel like playing
with a dog? That will make
him think you do want to play.
The better thing to do is to
cross your arms and turn
around. That means: "I don't
feel like playing, dog. Go and
play with someone else."

Puppies

A baby dog is called a puppy. Dogs give birth to more than one puppy at a time. Sometimes as many as fifteen. They grow inside the mother's belly. When they are born they are bald, wriggling animals and they look a bit like little rats.

Two weeks after they're born puppies open their eyes. The puppies drink milk from their mother. If the mother doesn't have enough milk the puppies can be fed milk from a bottle. When they're two months old they are ready to go to their new homes.

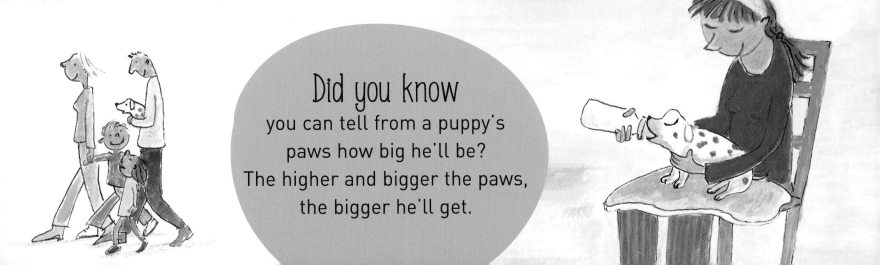

Did you know
you can tell from a puppy's paws how big he'll be? The higher and bigger the paws, the bigger he'll get.

The dog doctor

A dog has to go to the dog doctor, called a vet, every year.
The vet will check to see if the dog is healthy. Is he growing well? Does he have fleas?
Dogs also get shots so they don't get sick.

Did you know
sick dogs sometimes
have to stay at the
vet's office?
It's like staying
in dog hospital.

Sometimes dogs get sick. Of course they can't tell you that they aren't feeling well.
Luckily you can tell. If your dog doesn't want to eat, play or go outside for a walk,
then he's probably ill. Because all dogs love eating and playing and going outside.

RING 2

RING 1

DOG FOOD

2

1

3

The prettiest, the very prettiest
gets a prize – and an extra dog treat.

The dog show

Who has the prettiest dog at the show?
The proud owners show their dogs.

A judge decides who wins.
He pays attention to the dog's
teeth. To the dog's shape and
the way the dog walks.

The dogs walk around the ring.
They each have a number,
so the judge knows exactly
which dog is which. Which
one do you like best?

The big fancy dog show
with Lana and Duffy

Grandpa is in a good mood.
"Come on," he calls. "We are
going to dress up Duffy for
the dog show. Where is she?"

Lana has no idea.
Duffy is not in her basket.

She's not in the closet either.

She's not behind the curtains.
Not under the table.
Not in the washing machine.

"Aha, here she is," Lana cries.
Duffy is in the backyard. And she
is dirty! She is covered in mud.
"That's alright," Grandpa says.
"We will make her look
pretty again."

Grandpa cuts her hair.

Lana gives her a bath.

Grandpa does her nails.

Lana brushes her teeth.

Grandpa combs her hair.

"A real lady,"
Grandpa says proudly.
"Duffy is the prettiest dog in
all the land. You'll see."

At the dog show there is also a dog shop where you can buy all sorts of things for your dog. Baskets, leashes, brushes, bows and toothbrushes. For small dogs that can't walk very far there are even dog buggies.

Did you know some people buy clothes for their dogs? Dresses and coats, hats and caps? Even bows! How many red bows do you see?

The owners try their hardest to make their dogs look pretty. They cut and comb and blow-dry until their dogs look perfect.

How many kinds of dogs are there?

There are a lot of different dogs. Big ones and small ones. Long haired and short haired, floppy eared and pointy eared. There are dogs that are super fast. There are tough, strong, sweet and smart dogs. Some people say that a dog's owner looks a lot like his or her dog.

Bulldog
the toughest dog
(he loves fighting).

Shar-Pei
have you ever seen
a dog with this
many wrinkles?

Chinese crested dog
this little dog has
almost no hair.

Chihuahua
the smallest (as small as a rabbit).

Working dogs

Some dogs are so smart that they can help humans. Did you know that there are dogs with real professions? Of course there are no dentists, teachers or bus drivers.

Guard dogs guard houses and offices. They watch over things, bark loudly, and are good fighters.

Sheepdogs help shepherds to keep the flock together.

Hounds have excellent noses and can run very fast. They help hunters during the hunt.

Police dogs have keen noses, and help the police to find and catch criminals.

Guide dogs show blind people or people with poor vision where to go.

Did you know one of the first animals in space was a dog? Her name was Laika.

Rescue dogs look for people who need help. They wear small barrels that contain warm drinks around their necks.

Circus dogs know a lot of tricks. They can dance, walk around on their hind legs and jump through hoops.

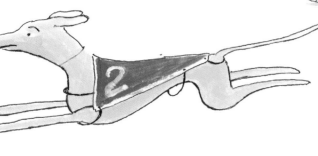

Race dogs participate in dog races. Greyhounds are the fastest of all dogs. They run faster than tigers.

Some dogs can act so well they get to work in the movies.

Sled dogs are strong enough to pull a sled filled with people.

Little doggies

(To the tune of "Ten Little Indians")

One little, two little, three little doggies,
Four little, five little, six little doggies,
Seven little, eight little, nine little doggies,
Come and play with me.

Nine little, eight little, seven little doggies,
Six little, five little, four little doggies,
Three little, two little,
ONE little doggie.
Please will you be mine?

Make your own dog mask!

This is what you need:

- Wallpaper paste
- Measuring cup
- Bowl
- Newspaper torn into strips
- Balloon
- Paint
- Colored paper or cloth
- Small paper cup

This is what you do:

 1. Make the wallpaper paste following the instructions on the box and put it in the bowl.

 2. Blow up the balloon. Cover one half of the balloon with strips of paper that have been dipped in the paste.

 3. Paste a cardboard cup on the balloon to make a snout. Paste strips of newspaper over the cup.

 4. When the mask is dry, you can break the balloon.

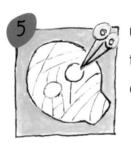 5. Cut holes in the mask for eye holes.

 6. Paint the mask. You can use colored cloth or paper to make ears.

So many lovely dogs!

Mini-quiz

1. What color can't a dog see?

2. Which dog is as tall as you?

3. What do dogs do when they are angry?

4. What are dogs absolutely not allowed to eat?

5. What do dogs do when they meet other dogs?

6. How many times a day do you have to walk a dog?

7. How many puppies can a dog have?

8. How can you teach a dog to do something?

9. What does a dog not need?

10. Why is it not good for a dog to sleep in his owner's bed?